THE LITTLE BOOK OF

DOGS

Published by OH!
20 Mortimer Street
London W1T 3JW

ISBN 978-1-91161-095-3

Editorial: Stella Caldwell
Project manager: Russell Porter
Design: Tony Seddon
Production: Rachel Burgess

A CIP catalogue record for this book is available from the British Library

Printed in Dubai

10 9 8 7 6 5 4 3 2 1

Illustrations: Shutterstock

THE LITTLE BOOK OF
DOGS

WOOFS OF WISDOM

CONTENTS

INTRODUCTION – 6

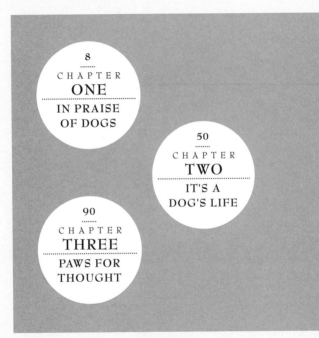

8
......
CHAPTER
ONE
......
IN PRAISE
OF DOGS

50
......
CHAPTER
TWO
IT'S A
DOG'S LIFE

90
......
CHAPTER
THREE
PAWS FOR
THOUGHT

104

CHAPTER
FOUR

MAN'S BEST
FRIEND

158

CHAPTER
FIVE

WOOF
WISDOM

INTRODUCTION

FROM poodles and Pomeranians to Alsatians and Afghan hounds, dogs have been our loyal companions for thousands of years. They live with us, work with us, play with us – and yes, sometimes they even share our beds.

We can't be sure when exactly wild wolves became dogs living alongside people. The earliest known grave containing both human and dog remains was discovered in 1914, in Germany. Researchers concluded the grave's occupants – a man, a woman and a puppy – were buried at least 14,000 years ago, in the Paleolithic era. Recently, new studies have shown that not only was the puppy domesticated, it also seems to have been well cared for. In other words, there was an emotional bond between man and dog.

But whenever domestication happened, and however it happened – because some scientists argue that wolves approached humans rather than the other way round! – there is no denying that it was the start of a highly successful relationship between people and dogs. Wolves not only developed floppy ears and wagging tails, but also the incredible ability to tune into human gestures and emotions. As pack loyalty became devotion to a human master, dogs discovered their own way of communicating with us. Our pooches cry when we leave the house, and joyfully greet our return – and the unconditional love they show us adds up to a lot more than just looking for shelter or food.

Whether bounding across a muddy field, rounding up sheep, gleefully chasing the neighbour's cat, or excitedly greeting us at the door, dogs really are man's best friend – and like any good friend, they can teach us something about ourselves.

The perfect gift for any dog-lover, this Little Book contains fascinating snippets of information about our furry friends, and is packed full of wonderful quotes and perfectly pawsome wit and wisdom.

CHAPTER
ONE

IN PRAISE OF DOGS

People and dogs have lived together for at least

14,000

years.

"**D**ogs are such agreeable friends. They ask no questions, they make no criticisms."

George Eliot

"Near this spot
Are deposited the Remains of one
Who possessed Beauty without
     Vanity,
Strength without Insolence,
Courage without Ferocity,
And all the virtues of Man, without
     his Vices.

This Praise, which would be
    unmeaning Flattery
If inscribed over human ashes,
Is but a just tribute to the
    Memory of
BOATSWAIN, a DOG."

Lord Byron, "Epitaph to a Dog", written in
memory of his Newfoundland dog, Botswain,
who died of rabies, 1808

Dachshunds and
Dalmatians may not look
the part, but all dogs are
descended from

grey
wolves.

"A dog's spirit dies hard."

Mikhail Bulgakov, *Heart of a Dog*, 1925

"The more one comes to know men, the more one comes to admire the dog."

Marie de Rabutin-Chantal, marquise de Sévigné

"If you pick up a starving dog and make him prosperous, he will not bite you. This is the principal difference between a dog and a man.**"**

Mark Twain, *Pudd'nhead Wilson*, 1894

❝I believe that a dog brings out the very best there is in man or woman. Dogs make me feel how shabby most of our loyalties are, how limited our patience, how destructible our love of one another… You couldn't revert to the savage state so easily if you had a dog on a desert island. For a dog is a gentleman, with kindliness in his heart and dignity in his demeanour…"

Kay Francis, "If I Were Marooned on a Desert Island", by Faith Service in *Picturegoer*, 27 March 1937

Having a dog
will bless you with
the

happiest

days of
your life, and one
of the

worst

days.

"**I**f you eliminate smoking and gambling, you will be amazed to find that almost all an Englishman's pleasures can be, and mostly are, shared by his dog."

George Bernard Shaw

The fastest dog,
the greyhound, can run
up to

44 miles
(71 km)

per hour.

"Our perfect companions never have fewer than four feet."

Colette

"Some of our greatest historical and artistic treasures we place with curators in museums; others we take for walks."

Roger A. Caras

If the kindest souls
were rewarded with the

longest lives,

dogs

would
outlive us all.

"No matter how little money and how few possessions you own, having a dog makes you rich."

Louis Sabin

> "I love a dog. He does nothing for political reasons."

Will Rogers

Home is where the dog runs to greet you.

"Happiness is a warm puppy."

Charles M. Schulz

Dogs' wet noses

help them to smell better.

The wetness is due to a mixture of mucus and saliva, which helps to trap tiny scent particles.

"Dogs never bite me.
Just humans.**"**

Marilyn Monroe, as quoted in Truman Capote,
Music for Chameleons, 1980

"**S**ome of my best leading men have been dogs and horses."

Elizabeth Taylor, *The Times*, 1981

"I think dogs are the most amazing creatures; they give unconditional love. For me, they are the role models for being alive.**"**

Gilda Radner

"I like dogs. You always know what a dog is thinking. It has four moods. Happy, sad, cross and concentrating. Also, dogs are faithful and they do not tell lies because they cannot talk."

Mark Haddon, *The Curious Incident of the Dog in the Night-time*, 2003

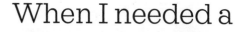

When I needed a
hand,
I found a
paw!

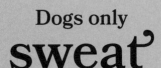

Dogs only **sweat** through footpads on their paws. The main way they cool down is by **panting,** allowing moisture to evaporate and lower the body temperature.

"Dogs eat with gusto, play with exuberance, work happily when given the opportunity, surrender themselves to the wonder and the mystery of their world, and love extravagantly."

Dean Koontz, *A Big Little Life:*
A Memoir of a Joyful Dog, 2009

"If I could be half the person my dog is, I'd be twice the human I am."

Charles Yu, *How to Live Safely in a Science Fictional Universe: A Novel*, 2010

Life is too *short* to have just **one** dog.

According to
Sir Paul McCartney,
the Beatles song

"A Day in the Life"

has a high frequency
whistle sound that
only dogs can hear.

Play it and
watch your dog!

"Even the tiniest
poodle or Chihuahua is
still a wolf at heart."

Dorothy Hinshaw

"**D**id you know that
there are over three hundred
words for love in canine?"

Gabrielle Zevin

"You know, a dog can snap you out of any kind of bad mood that you're in faster than you can think of."

Jill Abramson

"If you live with dogs, you'll never run out of things to write about."

Sharon Delarose

Dogs leave pawprints on our hearts

"Because dogs live in the present. Because dogs don't hold grudges. Because dogs let go of all their anger daily, hourly, and never let it fester. They absolve and forgive with each passing minute. Every turn of a corner is the opportunity for a clean slate. Every bounce of a ball brings joy and the promise of a fresh chase."

Stephen Rowley

"The dog is the perfect portrait subject. He doesn't pose. He isn't aware of the camera."

Patrick Demarchelier

The Norwegian

Lundehunde

has

six toes

on each foot.

"Money can buy you a fine dog but only love can make him wag his tail."

Kinky Friedman

··

CHAPTER

TWO

IT'S
A
DOG'S
LIFE

"A cat may be taught not to do certain things, but if it is caught out and flees, it flees not from shame, but from fear. But the shame of a dog touches an abyss of misery as bottomless as any human emotion. He has fallen out of the state of grace, and nothing but the absolution and remission of his sin will restore him to happiness."

Alfred George Gardiner, "A Dithyramb on a Dog", *Leaves in the Wind*, 1920

"You think those dogs will not be in heaven! I tell you they will be there long before any of us."

Robert Louis Stevenson

Dogs see
green,
yellow
and **blue**
like we do, but their
eyes can't process
red,
which they see
as dark grey.

"**I**n times of joy, all of us wished we possessed a tail we could wag."

W. H. Auden

"I've always tried out my material on my dogs first. Years ago, when my red setter chewed up the manuscript of *Of Mice and Men*, I said at the time that the dog must have been an excellent literary critic."

John Steinbeck

"I never married because there was no need. I have three pets at home, which answer the same purpose as a husband. I have a dog which growls every morning, a parrot which swears all afternoon, and a cat that comes home late at night."

Marie Corelli

Dogs don't always

 BARK

at night... but
when they do, you
can be sure it's for
no particular reason.

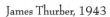

"The dog has seldom been successful in pulling Man up to its level of sagacity, but Man has frequently dragged the dog down to his."

James Thurber, 1943

MRI scans of
dogs' brains have shown
that they respond with
joy to pictures of
their owners.

Dogs
really do
love people!

"**A** dog cannot relate his autobiography; however eloquently he may bark, he cannot tell you that his parents were honest but poor."

Bertrand Russell, *Human Knowledge: Its Scope and Limits*, 1948

A well-trained
dog will make

no attempt

to share your
lunch – he will just
make you feel

so guilty

that you
cannot enjoy it.

"Scratch a dog and you'll find a permanent job."

Franklin P. Jones

"That flaming dog has messed on our steps again. It's the one species I wouldn't mind seeing disappear from the face of the earth. I wish they were like the white rhino – six of them left in the Serengeti National Park, and all males."

George in Alan Bennett's *Getting On*, 1971

"**A** dog will make eye contact. A cat will, too, but a cat's eyes don't even look entirely warm-blooded to me, whereas a dog's eyes look human except less guarded."

Roy Blount Jr, "Dogs Vis-à-Vis Cats",
Now, Where Were We?, 1989

Dogs are nature's remedy for a **bad** hair day.

"A dog's got personality. Personality goes a long way."

Quentin Tarantino, *Pulp Fiction*, 1994

Bluey, an Australian
cattle dog, lived from
1910 until 1939 –
an incredible

29 years and five months.

"Dogs' lives are too short. Their only fault, really."

Agnes Sligh Turnbull

"My fashion philosophy is, if you're not covered in dog hair, your life is empty."

Elayne Boosler

"If you think dogs can't count, try putting three dog biscuits in your pocket and then give Fido only two of them."

Phil Pastoret

My dog
is not
disobedient,
just
spontaneous.

"If you have a dog, you will most likely outlive it; to get a dog is to open yourself to profound joy and, prospectively, to equally profound sadness."

Marjorie Garber

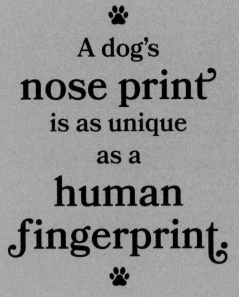

A dog's **nose print** is as unique as a **human fingerprint.**

"**I** wonder if other dogs think poodles are members of a weird religious cult."

Rita Rudner

My dog thinks I'm a

catch.

"**D**id you ever walk into
a room and forget why you
walked in? I think that is
how dogs spend their lives."

Sue Murphy

Just like their wolf
ancestors, dogs sometimes

howl

when they are
alone as a way of
looking for

company.

"The greatest fear dogs know is the fear that you will not come back when you go out the door without them."

Stanley Coren

"A dog desires affection more than its dinner. Well – almost."

Charlotte Gray

Dogs have
so many friends
because they

WAG

their tails,
not their tongues.

"Useful commands to teach your dog are 'Stay', 'Heel', 'Remove your snout from that person's groin', 'Stop humping the Barcalounger', 'Do not bark violently for two hours at inanimate objects such as a flowerpot', 'Do not eat poop', and 'If you must eat poop, then at least refrain from licking my face afterwards'."

Dave Barry, *I'll Mature When I'm Dead: Dave Barry's Amazing Tales of Adulthood*, 2011

"**D**ogs feel very strongly that they should always go with you in the car, in case the need should arise for them to bark violently at nothing right in your ear."

Dave Barry

Anybody
who doesn't know
what

soap

tastes like never
washed a

dog

"Dogs die. But dogs live, too. Right up until they die, they live. They live brave, beautiful lives. They protect their families. And love us, and make our lives a little brighter, and they don't waste time being afraid of tomorrow."

Dan Gemeinhart, *The Honest Truth*, 2015

"Owners of dogs will have noticed that, if you provide them with food and water and shelter and affection, they will think you are God. Whereas owners of cats are compelled to realize that, if you provide them with food and water and shelter and affection, they draw the conclusion that they are gods."

Christopher Hitchens, *The Portable Atheist: Essential Readings for the Nonbeliever*, 2007

"My dog is half pit-bull, half poodle. Not much of a watchdog, but a vicious gossip."

Craig Shoemaker

Scientists say a dog's sense of

smell

is anywhere from

10,000 to 100,000

times better than a human's.
Their super snouts can
detect the equivalent of half
a teaspoon of sugar in an
Olympic-sized swimming pool!

"**P**ercy does not like it when I read a book.

He puts his face over the top of it, and moans…

'Books?' says Percy. 'I ate one once, and it was enough. Let's go.'"

Mary Oliver, "Percy and Books", *Red Bird*, 2008

CHAPTER

THREE

PAWS
FOR
THOUGHT

Dogs are man's best friend —
and what are friends for, if not
to lend a hand (paw), and teach
us something about ourselves?

Watch how dogs interact
with the world and people
around them, and learn some
important life lessons....

Take time to smell the roses

Ever noticed how a dog will stop mid-sprint to luxuriate in that glorious (OK, possibly foul) smell?

Take time out of your busy schedule to enjoy the little things that make you happy.

Don't be afraid to get your paws dirty

Whether shredding a newspaper or getting caked in mud, dogs know that messy play is the best fun EVER.

Love someone? Let them know...

Dogs don't hold back when it comes to showing affection. A joyful bark, a slobbery lick or a snuggle on the sofa – spread the love!

Don't hold grudges

Your dog will never stay
mad at you for accidentally
stepping on his paw or
forgetting his bedtime
treat. Let go of your
grudges and be free.

Accept treats

A dog may not stick to the "everything in moderation" rule, but the occasional tasty treat can't be a bad thing!

Show compassion

Ever noticed how when you're feeling blue, your dog will comfort you with a wet nose kiss or a gentle lick? Showing someone you care doesn't have to be about grand gestures — sometimes, just being there is enough.

Greet people with enthusiasm

Dogs are quick to love and slow to judge – greet friends, neighbours and even complete strangers with a friendly smile and a cheery hello, and you might make their day.

Love unconditionally

No matter what mood you're in, your dog will be pleased to see you — and that wagging tail and wet nose will let you know about it. That's love.

Be loyal

Dogs stick with their pack
through thick and thin –
they run with their pack,
play with their pack and
defend their pack. Being a
loyal friend will add to your
life in many ways.

Always be yourself

Wouldn't it be dull if all dogs looked exactly the same and didn't have their own particular quirks? Dalmatians don't aspire to be sausage dogs and poodles don't dream of being Alsatians. Accept yourself the way you are.

Live in the moment

Just watch a dog bounding joyfully through a park and you will have an idea of what it is to live in the here and now. The past is past and the future is unknown — so make the best of what you have right now.

CHAPTER

FOUR

MAN'S
BEST
FRIEND

"Histories are more full of examples of the fidelity of dogs than of friends."

Alexander Pope, 1709.

"There are three faithful
friends, an old wife, an old
dog, and ready money."

Benjamin Franklin, *Poor Richard's Almanack*, 1734

Top 5 Brainiest Breeds

1. Border collie
2. Poodle
3. German shepherd
4. Golden retriever
5. Doberman

"You ask of my companions. Hills, Sir, and the sundown, and a dog as large as myself that my father bought me. They are better than human beings, because they know but do not tell."

Poet Emily Dickinson in a letter to
Thomas Wentworth Higginson, 1862

There is no
therapy
in the world like
a puppy

licking

your face.

"The love of a dog for his master is notorious; in the agony of death he has been known to caress his master..."

Charles Darwin, *The Descent of Man*, 1871

"The one absolutely unselfish friend that man can have in this selfish world, the one that never deserts him, the one that never proves ungrateful or treacherous is his dog. A man's dog stands by him in prosperity and in poverty, in health and in sickness. He will kiss the hand that has no food to offer…

… He will lick the wounds and sores that come in encounters with the roughness of the world. He guards the sleep of his pauper master as if he were a prince. When all other friends desert, he remains."

Senator George Graham Vest,
Eulogy on the Dog, c.1855

There's a reason
dogs and tots get along
so well – the average
dog is as smart as
a two year-old child,
and can understand
roughly

250

words and gestures.

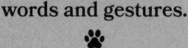

"**W**e are alone, absolutely alone on this chance planet: and, amid all the forms of life that surround us, not one, excepting the dog, has made an alliance with us."

Maurice Maeterlinck, *My Dog*, 1906

Love is a
four-legged
word.

"The greatest pleasure of a
dog is that you may make
a fool of yourself with him,
and not only will he not
scold you, but he will make
a fool of himself, too."

Samuel Butler, *The Notebooks of
Samuel Butler*, 1912

"When the Man waked up he said, 'What is Wild Dog doing here?' And the Woman said, 'His name is not Wild Dog any more, but the First Friend, because he will be our friend for always and always and always.'"

Rudyard Kipling, "The Cat that Walked by Himself", *Just So Stories*, 1902

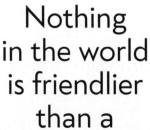

Nothing
in the world
is friendlier
than a

dog.

Although they are
born deaf,
dogs can hear

four times

better
than humans.

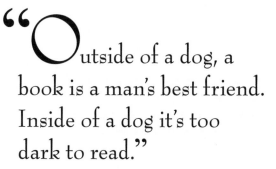

"Outside of a dog, a book is a man's best friend. Inside of a dog it's too dark to read."

Groucho Marx, *The Essential Groucho: Writings For, By and About Groucho Marx*, 2008

Whoever
said that
diamonds
are a girl's
best friend never
owned a dog.

"The truth I do not
stretch or shove
When I state that the dog
is full of love.
I've also found, by actual test,
A wet dog is the lovingest."

Ogden Nash, "The Dog"

It's no
coincidence
that man's
best friend
cannot

"The love of a dog is a pure thing. He gives you a trust that is total. You must not betray it."

Michel Houellebecq

"There is sorrow enough in the
natural way
From men and women to fill our day;
But when we are certain of sorrow
in store
Why do we always arrange for more?
Brothers and sisters I bid you beware
Of giving your heart to a dog to tear."

Rudyard Kipling, "The Power of the Dog", 1922

"A dog is the only thing on earth that loves you more than he loves himself."

Josh Billings

"To his dog, every man is Napoleon; hence the constant popularity of dogs."

Aldous Huxley, *Readers Digest*, 1934

"My little dog – a
heartbeat at my feet."

Edith Wharton

Dalmatian
puppies are born
pure white
and develop their
trademark

spots

as they
grow older.

"Like many other much-loved humans, they believed that they owned their dogs, instead of realizing that their dogs owned them."

Dodie Smith, *The 101 Dalmatians*, 1956

"The friendship of a dog is precious. It becomes even more so when one is so far removed from home... I have a Scottie. In him I find consolation and diversion... He is the one 'person' to whom I can talk without the conversation coming back to war."

Dwight D. Eisenhower, Supreme Commander of the Allied Expeditionary Force in Europe, in a letter to his wife, Mamie, 1943

"**W**hen a man's best friend is his dog, that dog has a problem."

Edward Abbey

*One reason a dog
can be such a comfort
when you're feeling*

BLUE

*is that
he doesn't try
to find out why.*

"The dog didn't care what I looked like, or what I did for a living, or what a train wreck of a life I'd led before I got her... She just wanted to be with me, and that awareness gave me a singular sensation of delight."

Caroline Knapp, *Pack of Two: the Intricate Bond Between People and Dogs*, 1999

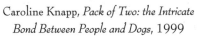

The basenji,
a hunting dog that
originated in
Africa, can't bark
but that doesn't
mean it's silent – it

yodels!

"dog's good for filling a grief-dug hole."

Eileen Granfors

"It seems to me that the good Lord in his infinite wisdom gave us three things to make life bearable – hope, jokes and dogs. But the greatest of these was dogs."

Robyn Davidson, *Tracks: A Woman's Solo Trek Across 1,700 Miles of Australian Outback*, 1995

A new dog
never replaces
an old dog.
It merely

expands

the heart.

With its waterproof coat and webbed feet, the mighty Newfoundland was originally bred to help fishermen

haul nets

and rescue people from

drowning.

"Dogs have a way of finding the people who need them."

Thom Jones

"I have caught more ills from people sneezing over me and giving me virus infections than from kissing dogs."

Barbara Woodhouse

A dog doesn't care if you're **rich** or **poor**, **smart** or **dumb**. Give him your heart... and he'll give you his.

"You call to a dog and a dog will break its neck to get to you. Dogs just want to please. Call to a cat and its attitude is, 'What's in it for me?'"

Lewis Grizzard

"I have found that when you are deeply troubled, there are things you get from the silent devoted companionship of a dog that you can get from no other source."

Doris Day

"**D**ogs are our link to paradise. They don't know evil or jealousy or discontent."

Milan Kundera, quoted in Doug Gelbert,
The Canine Hiker's Bible, 2000

"Nobody can fully understand the meaning of love unless he's owned a dog. A dog can show you more honest affection with a flick of his tail than a man can gather through a lifetime of handshakes."

Gene Hill

Without a dog, my *wallet* would be *full* and my *house* would be *clean*... but my heart would be empty.

"Not Carnegie, Vanderbilt and Astor together could have raised money enough to buy a quarter share in my little dog."

Ernest Thompson Seton

The bloodhound
has such a
reliable sense of smell
that its

evidence

can be presented
in some

courts of law.

"Dogs have a depth of loyalty that often we seem unworthy of."

Kinky Friedman, *Elvis, Jesus and Coca Cola*, 1994

"May I tell you a wonderful truth about your dog?... You have been given stewardship of what you in your faith might call a holy soul."

Dean Koontz, *A Big Little Life: A Memoir of a Joyful Dog*, 2009

"When an eighty-five pound mammal licks your tears away, then tries to sit on your lap, it's hard to feel sad."

Kristan Higgins

"A dog is the only thing that can mend a crack in your broken heart."

Judy Desmond

**_Love_ me,
love _my dog_**.

"When we adopt a dog or any pet, we know it is going to end with us having to say goodbye, but we still do it. And we do it for a very good reason: They bring so much joy and optimism and happiness. They attack every moment of every day with that attitude."

W. Bruce Cameron

"It's tough to stay married. My wife kisses the dog on the lips, yet she won't drink from my glass."

Rodney Dangerfield

CHAPTER

FIVE

WOOF
WISDOM

"The dog lives for the day, the hour, even the moment."

Robert Falcon Scott , writing in his journal
during the South Pole expedition, 1911

"It's funny how dogs and cats know the inside of folks better than other folks do, isn't it?**"**

Eleanor H. Porter, *Pollyanna*, 1912

The *best* therapist has *fur* and *four legs.*

"A bone to the dog is not charity. Charity is the bone shared with the dog when you are just as hungry as the dog."

Jack London, "Confession", 1912

"A boy can learn a lot from a dog: obedience, loyalty, and the importance of turning around three times before lying down."

Robert Benchley, *Liberty* Magazine, 1932

Keep calm and pet a dog.

Rin Tin Tin,
a German
shepherd dog, was rescued
from a World War One
battlefield and went on to
star in 27

Hollywood
films.

"If a dog will not come to you after he has looked you in the face, you ought to go home and examine your conscience."

Woodrow Wilson

Everyone
thinks
they have the
best dog – and
nobody
is wrong...

"Just give me a comfortable couch, a dog, a good book and a woman. Then if you can get the dog to go somewhere and read the book, I might have a little fun."

Groucho Marx

The beautiful Saluki (Persian hound) is one of the oldest breeds of dog, and has been found depicted in rock art dating back at least

6,000

years.

"I've seen a look in dogs'
eyes, a quickly vanishing
look of amazed contempt,
and I am convinced that
basically dogs think humans
are nuts.**"**

John Steinbeck

If you want
the best seat
in the house,
you'll have to

the dog.

"A dog reflects the family life. Whoever saw a frisky dog in a gloomy family, or a sad dog in a happy one? Snarling people have snarling dogs, dangerous people have dangerous ones."

Arthur Conan Doyle, *The Case-Book of Sherlock Holmes*, 1927

ZZZ

Let sleeping dogs *lie*.

"There is no faith which has never yet been broken, except that of a truly faithful dog."

Konrad Lorenz

Whoever said you
can't buy
happiness
forgot
about puppies.

"Dogs are wise. They crawl away into a quiet corner and lick their wounds and do not rejoin the world until they are whole once more."

Agatha Christie, *The Moving Finger*, 1942

"Dogs can never speak the language of humans, and humans can never speak the language of dogs. But many dogs can understand almost every word humans say, while humans seldom learn to recognize more than half a dozen barks, if that."

Dodie Smith, *The 101 Dalmatians*, 1956

"**D**ogs do speak, but only to those who know how to listen."

Orhan Pamuk, *My Name is Red*, 1998

To err is
human
– to forgive,
canine.

"**B**e the person your dog thinks you are."

C.J. Frick

The average number
of puppies in a litter is
six to **ten.**
That means that just
one female dog and
her offspring can
theoretically produce
67,000
puppies over six years.

"Don't accept your dog's admiration as conclusive evidence that you are wonderful."

Ann Landers

My **goal** in life
is to be
as **good** a person
as my dog
thinks I am.

"**W**hy does watching a dog be a dog fill one with happiness? And why does it make one feel, in the best sense of the word, human?"

Jonathan Safran Foer, *New York Times*, 2006

"Marley taught me about living each day with unbridled exuberance and joy, about seizing the moment. He taught me to appreciate the simple things — a walk in the woods, a fresh snowfall, a nap in a shaft of winter sunlight. And as he grew old and achy, he taught me about optimism in the face of adversity…

… Mostly, he taught me about friendship and selflessness and, above all else, unwavering loyalty."

John Grogan, *Marley and Me: Life and Love With the World's Worst Dog*, 2005

Petting your dog
lowers
your
blood pressure
– and your dog's too!

"**D**ogs don't rationalize. They don't hold anything against a person. They don't see the outside of a human but the inside of a human."

Cesar Millan

"The world would be a nicer place if everyone had the ability to love unconditionally as a dog."

M.K. Clinton, *Showstoppers*, 2013

"Folk will know how large your soul is, by the way you treat a dog."

Charles F. Doran

Everything
I know
I learned
from
DOGS.